Copyright © 2023 by Kari Lavelle
Cover and internal design © 2023 by Sourcebooks
Cover images © Alexander Wild. Chris Van Wyk. Getty: Kjersti Busk Joergensen;
MirageC; Norbert Probst; Stan Tekiela Author / Naturalist / Wildlife Photographer.
Mario Sacramento. Mohd Zaidi Razak/Alamy. Eric Isselee/Shutterstock.
Internal images © Alamy: BIOSPHOTO, Adam Fletcher; Daybreak Imagery;
Imaginechina Limited, Imaginechina; Mohd Zaidi Razak. Alexander Wild.
Chris Van Wyk. Getty: Fourleaflover; Kjersti Busk Joergensen; MirageC;
Norbert Probst; Stan Tekiela Author / Naturalist / Wildlife Photographer;
Vicki Smith. Mario Sacramento. orangkucing / http://orangkucing.tumblr
.com/, License: CC BY Attribution-ShareAlike. Eric Isselee/Shutterstock.
Illustrations by Michelle Mayhall/Sourcebooks

Sourcebooks and the colophon are registered trademarks of Sourcebooks.

Published by Sourcebooks eXplore, an imprint of Sourcebooks Kids
P.O. Box 4410, Naperville, Illinois 60567-4410
(630) 961-3900
sourcebookskids.com

Cataloging-in-Publication Data is on file with the Library of Congress.

Source of Production: 1010 Printing Asia Limited, Kwun Tong, Hong Kong, China
Date of Production: November 2023
Run Number: 5035999

Printed and bound in China.
OGP 10 9 8 7 6 5 4 3 2

BUTT or FACE?

Can you tell which end you're looking at?

KARI LAVELLE

sourcebooks
eXplore

From their heads to their tails, animals have evolved to thrive and survive in the wild. Just like you, they use their bodies and their senses to learn about the world around them.

How does your face help you? Your eyes, ears, lips, and nose are part of your senses: sight, hearing, taste, smell, and touch.

Now think about your butt. Are you sitting on yours right now? How else does your *gluteus maximus* help you? Without your bottom, you wouldn't be able to run and play and yes...poop!

Faces and butts are important for animals too. But sometimes nature has the silliest sense of humor and it's hard to tell what we are looking at. The animal kingdom is full of funny faces and funny butts!

Are you ready for a game? How sharp are your scientific observational skills? Can you tell which of these close-up photos are animal faces and which are animal butts?

Let's play BUTT or FACE!

Take a look at this photo.

Do you think this is a

BUTT or a FACE?

What do you observe?
It looks like someone is looking at us!

It's a BUTT!

When startled, the Cuyaba dwarf frog flips around and inflates its posterior to scare off predators. If the predator isn't already intimidated, the frog will then emit a sticky, stinky substance as its next defense. Better steer clear of this one!

Is it a
BUTT

or FACE?

What animal does it belong to?

It's a BUTT!

You thought it was a zebra, right? Surprise! It's an okapi! The stripes on the okapi's backside help to camouflage it in the dim sunlight of the rain forest. The striped pattern also helps young okapi calves follow their mothers when they're exploring their habitat.

BACKSIDE

Even though its stripes look like a zebra, the okapi is related to the giraffe. And just like the giraffe, it has a long, dark tongue.

BEYOND THE BACKSIDE

This endangered mammal is found in the forests of the Democratic Republic of Congo.

This one looks interesting.
What animal do you think it is?
And more importantly,

is this a

BUTT or FACE?

This is the FACE of a star-nosed mole!

While it doesn't see very well (especially in its dark habitat), its nose is very sensitive and has twenty-two "feelers" that it uses to search for prey. The star-nosed mole dines on fine delicacies such as worms, fish, and various insects. Its nose is so sensitive, it can detect one grain of salt in a pile of sand! Or one in a *mole*-ion!

Is it a **BUTT**

or a **FACE**?

What do you see here?

It's a BUTT!

The markings of this Promethea moth caterpillar's rear might be just coincidental cuteness or it might be another case of confusing predators. Either way, it's hard not to smile back at that adorable little tush!

Here's another one!

Is it a **BUTT**

or **FACE?**

This is the FACE of the Mary River turtle!

That mohawk look isn't from a punk rock lifestyle, but from the algae of the Mary River. *Turtle-y* awesome, dude!

What would you guess this is?

Is it a **BUTT**

or a

FACE?

This is the beautiful BUTT of the orchid mantis!

BEYOND THE BACKSIDE

This insect is found in the tropical forests of Southeast Asia.

It lives camouflaged among flowers, but don't let this beauty fool you. This bug is fierce! When pollinators like bees investigate this "flower," the orchid mantis attacks and eats them. This deceptive appearance helps the orchid mantis camouflage itself so that predators also think it's a flower, not a meal. It's a mistake pollinators will learn once and *flor-al*!

BEYOND THE BACKSIDE

An orchid mantis will even eat their own sibling if they get too close. Talk about sibling rivalry—yikes!

Let's try another one.
How would you describe this photo?

Do you think this is a

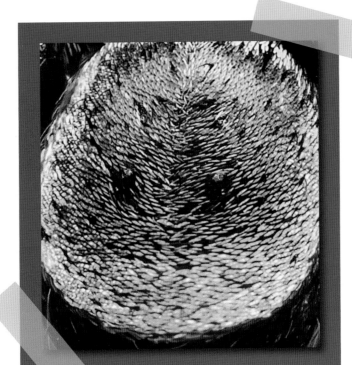

BUTT or a FACE?

It's a BUTT!

Male peacock spiders use this colorful pattern on their abdomen, along with an elaborate dance, to entice a mate. At this dance party, the male dances in front of the female for four to fifty minutes! And he better be good—if the female is not impressed, she might even eat the male! Maybe he should try the jitterbug!

BEYOND THE BACKSIDE

This spider species does not catch their food with a web. Instead, they stalk their prey before they jump on them!

BEYOND THE BACKSIDE

There are over ninety different species of peacock spiders (with different dances too!). And these arachnids have only been found in Australia!

Do you think it's a
BUTT

or
FACE?

What do you notice in this photo?

Can you believe it's part of the FACE of a proboscis monkey?

The word "proboscis" means "nose" and these animals have the biggest nose of all the primates. Male proboscis monkeys attract mates or scare off predators by making loud calls. Their noses create an echo chamber, amplifying the sound. You could say their noses *scent* those predators running!

FACE THE FACTS

Proboscis monkeys are great swimmers. If they race, one might easily win by a nose!

FACE THE FACTS

This mammal is found on the island of Borneo in southern Asia.

What about this photo?

Are you looking at

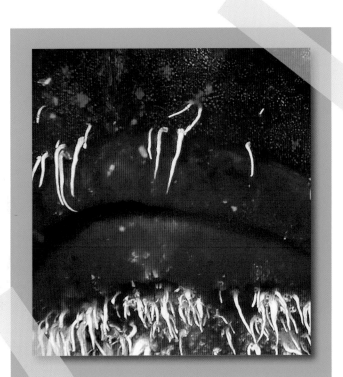

a BUTT or FACE?

Check out the FACE of this red-lipped batfish!

That rosy pout is all natural—no lipstick in this ocean! Scientists aren't exactly sure why these fish have such prominent lips, but most think it's to help them attract a mate.

FACE THE FACTS

This fish is found in the ocean around the Galápagos Islands.

FACE THE FACTS

Even though it's a fish, it's not a great swimmer. It actually uses its fins to waddle on the ocean floor.

This may look like an engraving on a piece of stone, but it's part of an animal. Can you guess what it is?

Is this a

BUTT or a FACE?

Ravine trapdoor spiders spend most of their lives inside their underground burrow.

This is the BUTT of a ravine trapdoor spider!

This arachnid uses its b
to blockade the entranc
home, keeping out pred:
like wasps. The ravine t
spider creates a burrow
underground with a tra
made of silk. It hides be
the trap door, waiting f
unsuspecting insect to
inside. If its visitor is a
wasp and not a delicious
option, the spider prese
shield-like bottom and
wasp from entering. But

This arachnid is found in the United States. Be on the lookout for these if you're exploring the ravines of Alabama, Tennessee, or Georgia.

Is it a
BUTT
or
FACE?

Some turtle ants also have the unusual ability of gliding. They're able to steer their bodies when they fall, almost like a rudder or parachute.

It's the FACE of the turtle ant! ●●

There are over a hundred species of turtle ants and they are found in the forests of Central and South America.

Some turtle ants use their giant heads to blockade the entrance of their homes, preventing any intruders from entering. Way to use your head, turtle ants!

Is this a

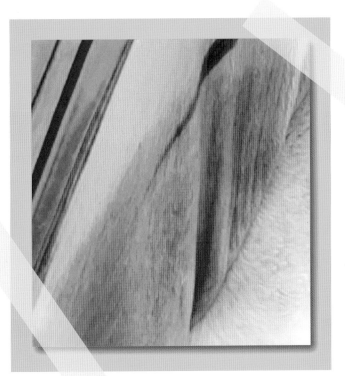

BUTT or a FACE?

It's the FACE of the Australian pelican.

FACE THE FACTS

The Australian pelican is found in Australia, New Guinea, Fiji, as well as parts of Indonesia and New Zealand.

They use their pouch to scoop up food, not store it. They catch fish by diving from the surface of the water. Sometimes they work together to drive fish to shallower waters, where it's easier to catch them. Any water drains out of its pouch before it swallows its meal whole!

FACE THE FACTS

This species has the longest bill of any bird on the planet—up to 18.5 inches (47 cm) long!

Do you feel like an expert now?
Try this last one.

Is this a BUTT

or a FACE?

Trick question!

It's the FACE of a pearlfish inside the BUTT of a sea cucumber!

Pearlfish are parasites that make their homes inside sea cucumbers. Sea cucumbers breathe through this opening, which also serves as the door to the pearlfish's home.

Animal identification can be tricky! The next time you observe wildlife, look again.

Appearances are not always what they seem—many animals have specific features that help them survive.

Living creatures use their faces to eat, smell, communicate, and protect themselves. Animal rear ends are more than just a way to move around, sit comfortably, or get rid of waste: they help to connect with a companion, confuse potential prey, and defend against predators.

By learning more about animals, we can help protect them and their habitats. In the animal world, sometimes your butt will save your face and your face just might save your butt!

AUTHOR'S NOTE

The idea for this book originated from an article I read about farmers in Botswana. Farmers paint eyes on the behinds of cattle to scare away predators, like lions. Painting the cattle helps the farmers keep their livestock safe. It also helps the lionesses—angry farmers were hunting the endangered species to protect their livestock. As I read the article, I thought about how the lionesses had to ask themselves "Is that a butt or a face?" when they approached the cattle, leading to the concept of this picture book.

FOURTH GRADE KARI

GROWN-UP KARI

Photo © Mary Beth Huerta

ABOUT THE AUTHOR

This is the FACE of Kari Lavelle as a fourth grader. Kari had so much fun sitting on her BUTT, learning wacky facts about animals and writing this book. She's also the author of *We Move the World*. Kari lives in Austin, Texas, with her husband, their two kids and their dog, Dobby (who has a very cute BUTT and FACE).

	WHERE THEY REST THEIR **BUTTS**	WHAT GOES IN THEIR **FACES** 
1. CUYABA DWARF FROG *Physalaemus nattereri*	Parts of South America (Brazil, Bolivia, and Paraguay)	Insects
2. MARY RIVER TURTLE *Elusor macrurus*	Around the Mary River in Australia	Mostly plants and the occasional fish or frog
3. TURTLE ANT *Cephalotes varians*	Forests of Central and South America, all the way north to Texas and Arizona	Nectar, pollen, fungi, and even other animals' excrement (a fancy word for poop)
4. OKAPI *Okapia johnstoni*	Forests of the Democratic Republic of Congo	45 to 60 pounds of plants every day
5. PEACOCK SPIDER *Maratus anomalus*	Australia	Any insects they can catch
6. PROBOSCIS MONKEY *Nasalis larvatus*	Island of Borneo in southern Asia	Leaves, fruits, seeds, and the occasional insect
7. RED-LIPPED BATFISH *Ogcocephalus darwini*	Ocean around the Galápagos Islands	Small fish, crabs, shrimp, and worms
8. RAVINE TRAPDOOR SPIDER *Cyclocosmia truncata*	Georgia, Alabama, Tennessee	Beetles, crickets, moths, and grasshoppers
9. STAR-NOSED MOLE *Condylura cristata*	The United States, as far south as Virginia and as far west as North Dakota	Worms, fish, and various insects
10. PROMETHEA MOTH CATERPILLAR *Callosamia promethea*	Along the eastern United States and as far west as the Great Plains	Leaves
11. ORCHID MANTIS *Hymenopus coronatus*	Tropical forests of Southeast Asia	Mostly other insects
12. AUSTRALIAN PELICAN *Pelecanus conspicillatus*	Australia, New Guinea, Fiji, parts of Indonesia, and New Zealand	Primarily fish
13. SEA CUCUMBER *Bohadschia argus*	Everywhere	Small sea creatures, algae and waste products
14. PEARLFISH *Encheliophis boraborensis*	Tropical regions of the Atlantic, Indian, and Pacific oceans	Small fish or crustaceans and sometimes the organs of sea cucumbers